TANTALLON

C J Tabraham BA, FSA Scot
Inspector of Ancient Monuments
From an original text by
the late **J S Richardson**
HRSA, LLD, FSA Scot

Series editor
David J Breeze BA, PhD, FSA, FSA Scot
Inspector of Ancient Monuments

Historic Buildings and Monuments
Scottish Development Department

Edinburgh
Her Majesty's Stationery Office

'Of suche strength'

antallon Castle is one of the most awesome sights in all Scotland. Boldly rising up from the rocky coastal fringe of the Firth of Forth, its broad, massive and high form is drawn across the grassy headland like a great red curtain of stone. On the remaining sides, the cliffs plunge downwards to the chilly waters far beneath. Ruined and uninhabited these past three centuries, Tantallon makes an unforgettable impression on everyone who sees it.

Small wonder then that, from the time of its construction in the fourteenth century and throughout its history as a mighty

> *. . . Tantallon vast,*
> *Broad, massive, high and stretching far,*
> *And held impregnable in war,*
> *On a projecting rock it rose,*
> *And round three sides the ocean flows.*
> (*Marmion*, Sir Walter Scott)

stronghold of the Douglas earls of Angus, Tantallon figured prominently in the nation's affairs. 'It is of suche strength as I nede not to feare the malice of myne enymeys', penned one of many who sought, and found, security behind its curtain wall.

Tantallon was among the last of the great baronial courtyard-castles to be built. Few were prepared to embark upon such expensive undertakings in the aftermath of the prolonged struggle against the English. Most Scottish noblemen were now demonstrating a preference for the less ambitious, less costly but equally secure defended residence, the tower house. The builder of Tantallon, on the other hand,

chose to look back to the great age of castle building.

Tantallon's master was Sir William Douglas, created first earl of Douglas in 1358. His ancestors, not significant landowners before the wars of independence, had gained enormously through their close association with Robert Bruce. By 1354, Sir William's new-found wealth and prestige may well have encouraged him to build an imposing residence befitting one who was among the foremost barons of his day.

In 1388, after the death of James, the second earl, the house of Douglas was divided into two branches — the 'Red' and the 'Black' Douglases — and the castle passed to George Douglas, illegitimate son of the first earl and his mistress, Margaret Stewart, countess of Angus. George acquired the earldom of Angus and it is with the Douglas earls of Angus, the 'Red' Douglases, that Tantallon is most closely associated. Whenever they were in conflict with the crown, which occurred regularly, Tantallon, as their chief seat, became a focus of attention, most notably in 1528, when the castle walls withstood a twenty-day bombardment from James V's artillery train.

When the king took possession, he initiated comprehensive repairs, rendering the castle 'unwinabill . . . to any enemies'. The castle saw further action thereafter, but nothing to compare with the 1528 siege.

Cromwell's investment of the castle by a substantial force in 1651 caused much of the ruination that we see today and, before that century was out, Tantallon was abandoned both as a residence and a fortress. It came into state care in 1924.

A tour of the castle begins on page 15 and a plan can be found on the inside back cover.

A watercolour of Tantallon by Lt Col Frances Charteris Davidson.(Reproduced by kind permission of the Royal Commission on the Ancient and Historical Monuments of Scotland)

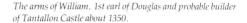
The arms of William, 1st earl of Douglas and probable builder of Tantallon Castle about 1350.

Family tree of the 'Red' Douglas earls of Angus.

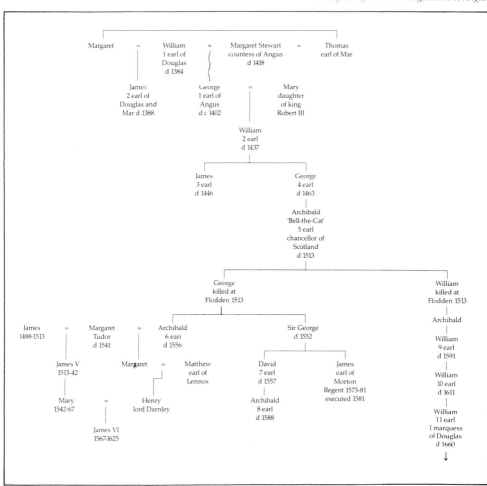

4

'Unwinabill...to any enemies'

Construction

Tantallon is an ancient placename but any evidence of an early fort, if such existed where Tantallon Castle now stands, has long since disappeared. In the early Middle Ages the barony of North Berwick was held by the Celtic earls of Fife, one of whom, Earl Duncan I, established a convent of Cistercian nuns there about 1150. Judging by the architectural details and in view of Tantallon's complete absence from the records charting the history of the wars of independence, the present castle was built around the middle of the fourteenth century, but it is not entirely clear who ordered its construction.

Two of the most influential aristocrats in the realm made rival claims to ownership. William, first earl of Douglas, wrote from 'our Castle of Temptaloun' in 1374, whilst Robert Stewart, earl of Fife and Menteith, claimed title to the lands and 'castel of Temtaloun' in 1388. Whoever the owner, it is clear that he would have had to be confident he had good, legal title to the estate before embarking upon such a costly building operation.

The only support for Robert Stewart's claim is a document issued by him following a visit he made to the castle after the death of James, second earl of Douglas. But, in the absence of corroborative documentation, and particularly in view of the fact that Robert Stewart is known to have had a propensity for depriving others of their own rights of inheritance in order to advance his own, his claim to the title must be considered dubious.

The earl of Douglas, on the other hand, could claim undisputed title to certain lands within the barony of North Berwick. In 1354, David II confirmed to William Douglas all the lands belonging to his father, Archibald, and his uncle, 'the Good' Sir James. They included 'Famyltoun and Bondingtoun' in the barony of North Berwick. 'Famyltoun' is no longer traceable; 'Bondingtoun' survives as Bonnington, a farm south of North Berwick Law. A charter dated 1452 grouped these two estates with 'Castiltoune and Halfpleuland', both still in existence in the immediate vicinity of the castle. Because of this we may confidently assume that a good part of the ancient barony of North Berwick had been taken from the earl of Fife and granted to Sir James Douglas, probably by Robert I in gratitude for services rendered during the struggle for independence.

The date of the building of the castle, the middle of the fourteenth century, coincides with the emergence of William Douglas as a powerful figure in political life. Having spent his youth in France, he returned to Scotland after the battle of Neville's Cross in 1346, only to discover his godfather and namesake, the infamous 'Knight of Liddesdale', blocking his rightful claim to the lordship of Douglas. In August 1353, godson waylaid godfather in the Ettrick Forest and killed him; thus William Douglas became undisputed overlord of the Scottish border country. By 1358 he was first earl of the mighty house of Douglas. With good title to the lands in the barony of North Berwick, and with his star very much in the ascendant, we can see his creation of this awe-inspiring fortress-residence as an undeniable statement of his power and prestige.

Tantallon and the 'Red' Douglases

Before the year 1357 William Douglas married Margaret, sister of Thomas, earl of Mar. Later, he made his brother-in-law's widow, who had assumed the title of countess of Angus and Mar, his mistress, and they both resided at Tantallon. To them was born a son, George Douglas, illegitimate and born in incest. William died in 1384, and his rightful son and heir, James, was killed four years later on the battlefield of Otterburn.

This unhappy turn of events may have prompted the avaricious Robert Stewart to attempt to regain title to the lands, but the countess of Angus proved too astute. At the parliament held in Holyrood Abbey on 9 April, 1389, she resigned her earldom of Angus in favour of her son, George Douglas. Within a short time, James Sandiland of Calder, heir of line to the unentailed Douglas estates, which included those in North Berwick, had been persuaded to grant his rights to George Douglas, the first Douglas earl of Angus, and so Tantallon Castle became the chief seat of the 'Red' Douglas earls of Angus.

George was captured by the English at the battle of Homildon and died in 1403 of an illness contracted during his captivity. His son William, the second earl, was among the Scottish nobles who, in April 1424, met James I at Durham after his long exile and escorted him into his own realm. In 1425 he was one of the lords who, under the presidency of the king, condemned Murdoch, duke of Albany, and his two sons, to the scaffold, and was responsible for the warding or imprisonment of the widowed duchess of Albany in Tantallon. While there, the duchess received an allowance from the Lord High Treasurer for dress and adornment. Four years later, Alexander, lord of the Isles, was imprisoned in the castle after he had done a humiliating penance at Holyrood 'dressed only in his shirt and drawers'.

James, the third earl, wielded great power and from his secure base at Tantallon he pursued his vendetta against the rival house of 'Black' Douglas as well as questioning the royal power. In 1445 he was summoned to appear before parliament or forfeit all his lands and goods and, following the plundering of his North Berwick barony, James sued for peace. He died shortly after.

The rivalry with the 'Black' Douglases was continued by the third earl's brother and heir, George, who in the 'Black' Douglas rebellion of 1455 received a high command in James II's army and, having completely routed the rebel forces at Arkinholm near Langholm, was rewarded with the lordship of Douglas. In August 1460 the earl was present at the siege of Roxburgh Castle and was slightly wounded by the cannon 'quhilk brak in the fyring' and killed the king. Seven days later, however, at Kelso Abbey, he had recovered sufficiently to place the crown upon the young King James III's head.

Earl George died in 1463 and his son Archibald succeeded him as the fifth earl. Better known in Scottish history as 'Bell-the-Cat' through his high-handed action at Lauder in 1482, he entered into a treasonable pact with Henry VII of England in 1491 to deliver James IV into English hands. Archibald was ordered to ward himself in his castle at Tantallon, but instead he chose to make preparations there for a lengthy siege. By October the king was before Tantallon. 'Quarioir the gunnar' was sent to Edinburgh

A gold ring (mid fifteenth century) found at Tantallon Castle. The ring is decorated with a male and female saint, enamelled flowers, and the initials JR. (In the collection of the Royal Museum of Scotland, Queen Street, Edinburgh: reproduced by kind permission of the National Museums of Scotland)

Castle to bring out the royal artillery train. Crossbows and culverins (a form of gun) were brought from Leith, and seamen were despatched in a boat to Largo, on the Fife coast, to bring the king's ship, *The Flower*, no doubt to blockade the castle from the sea. Items of expenditure recorded in the Lord High Treasurer's accounts show the king playing, and losing heavily, at cards as the investment of the castle continued. Quite how the siege ended we do not know, but the king was successful in bringing Archibald to book. The two would appear to have come to amicable terms, for the king was able to send his recalcitrant earl a Christmas present of 'a black velvet gown with lambs wool and with bukram to the tail of it'. The earl, however, forfeited all his power and influence upon the Border.

In 1513 Bell-the-Cat died of old age, at the same time as his two sons, George, master of Angus, and Sir William of Glenbervie, were struck down in the flower of their youth on the bloody field of Flodden. With the heir to the earldom dead, Bell-the-Cat's grandson, another Archibald, succeeded as the sixth earl of Angus. His first wife having died, in 1514 he married Queen Margaret Tudor, widow of James IV. It is with this 'young witless fool', as his uncle described him, that Tantallon Castle emerges from relative obscurity into the forefront of the national stage.

Tantallon under siege — 1528

The political machinations of the minority of the young James V, during which the various factions vied with one another for control of the king's person, are so complex that they cannot be gone into here. It is clear, however, that by 1524 the sixth earl of Angus was foremost among the nobles who advocated an alliance with England rather than France. In 1525 it had been agreed that the young king should be cared for by each of the leading nobles in turn, but, when the time came for Archibald to give him up in November of that year, he failed to do so. For the next three years the earl kept the king a virtual prisoner in Edinburgh and strengthened his hand by advancing his various kinsmen into positions of authority. Several attempts by others to 'rescue' the king failed but at last James V managed to escape in May 1528 and reach his mother in Stirling Castle. With the king beyond his reach, the earl's authority was greatly weakened and he withdrew from the capital to the safety of his own fortress at Tantallon.

The young king, now in his seventeenth year and in control of his own destiny, took immediate steps to cut the ground from beneath the earl's feet. Archibald was summoned to appear before parliament on a charge of treason and when he failed to do so was put to the horn. By October, the king was before the walls of Tantallon with a substantial force. The last instance of a Scottish nobleman seriously resisting the authority of the crown from within his own castle was about to take place.

There is evidence in Tantallon's fabric to suggest that Archibald had taken steps previously to strengthen his castle to make it better able to withstand the effects of cannon bombardment. The great curtain of red sandstone may have been protected from the outset by a massive bank and ditch placed some 100 metres in advance of the castle, but the earl may have built the traverse wall and the small round tower, both furnished with gunholes of early-sixteenth-century type, flanking the entrance gateway into the outer ward.

Against this formidable fortress the king brought to bear a sizeable battery comprising two great cannons, two great battards, two moyens, two double falcons and four quarter falcons, brought out from Dunbar Castle, along with four more falcons culled from elsewhere plus 'their powder and bullets and gunners for to use them'.

As the soldiers marched to the siege, it is said they beat on their drums a rhythm, 'Ding Doon Tantalloun, Ding Doon Tantalloun'. This is supposed to be the origin of the 'Scots' March'. But Tantallon was not to be 'dinged doon'. According to one authority, 'it was never ane hair the war (worse)' after the twenty-day siege.

There were a number of reasons for the blockade's failure, including a dire shortage of powder and shot. But it is not unreasonable to assume that the outer earthwork, which would have kept the besiegers' guns at a safe distance and soaked up the artillery bombardment intended for the more vulnerable castle walls, played a significant part.

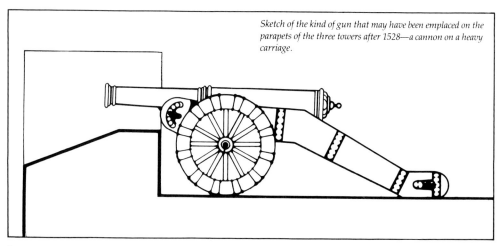

Sketch of the kind of gun that may have been emplaced on the parapets of the three towers after 1528—a cannon on a heavy carriage.

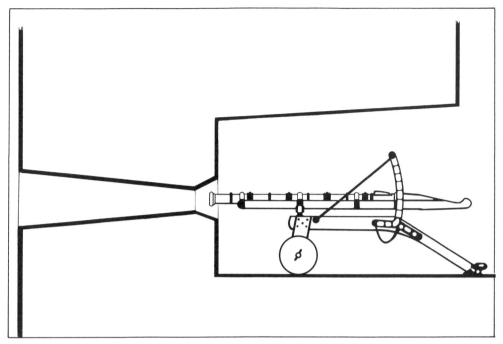

Sketch of the kind of gun that may have been used in the casemated gunholes in the lower storeys of the three towers—a stocked, forged-iron breech loader on a light trestle mounting.

Tantallon in crown hands

What the king could not wrest from his treacherous subject by force of arms he got through negotiation. By May of the following year, the sixth earl of Angus, for the second time in his villainous life, was in exile in England and Tantallon was delivered up to the king. The king, according to the contemporary historian, Robert Lindsay of Pitscottie, 'causit maissounis (masons) cum and rainforce samin wallis quhilk (which) was left waist of befoir as transses and throw passagis and maid all massie work to that effect that it sould be unwinabill in tymes comming to ony enemies that would come to persew it'. The truth of that statement is evident in the ruined castle today.

Between 1529 and the earl's return to Scotland from exile in 1543, soon after James V's death, the crown spent considerable sums on strengthening Tantallon's medieval defences. The mural stairs and chambers within the great curtain were infilled with masonry to render the walls more resistant to artillery bombardment. The wall-tops were refashioned with a crenellated parapet supported on continuous corbelling, suitable for hand-held guns resting on the crenels. The lofty towers terminating the curtain on either side were remodelled, strengthened and provided with gunholes, whilst the vulnerable gatehouse facade, previously furnished with a barbican, a defensive forework, in the later fourteenth or early fifteenth century, was substantially rebuilt and given a massive Fore Tower with rounded angles and large gunholes emplaced at strategic points. The outer defences were not neglected. The guntower and traverse wall flanking the outer gateway were repaired, and the ditch in front deepened, whilst the earthwork behind the outer ditch was, at least in part, given a masonry scarp wall.

Tantallon and the 'Rough Wooing'

With the earl returned from exile by 1543, and in full possession of his estates once more, his chief seat of Tantallon again became the focus of attention throughout Henry VIII of England's 'rough wooing' of the infant Mary Queen of Scots. Archibald was closely identified with the English king's cause, so much so that Henry wrote to his ambassador in Scotland, Sir Ralph Sadler, that he desired either Tantallon or Dunbar Castle as a place in which to keep his 'treasour', presumably the monies with which he bribed, or attempted to bribe, influential Scotsmen. And when hostilities broke out between the two nations, it was to Tantallon that Sadler opted to withdraw for his security. Archibald half-heartedly tried to dissuade the English ambassador from so doing, declaring the castle to 'be unfurnisshed and almoste all the lodginges taken downe to be newe buyldyd' — a reference no doubt to the recent upheaval caused by James V's alterations. Despite the lack of 'beddinge and all maner of householde stuff', Sadler moved in and thought himself 'nowe to be out of daungier'.

Sadler continued to defy Governor Arran's orders to quit the country and remained in Tantallon 'which is strong ynough to abyde . . . siege, and metely well furnisshed with artillery, but it is veray sclenderly furnisshed with vitaile, specially of wheate and malte, and also of cole, so that if we be besieged . . . we shall bothe lacke fyer and also be famysshed'. But the castle was not besieged, and with Sadler's ambassadorial overtures to the Scots replaced by the earl of Hertford's rapacious armies, Sadler slipped out of Tantallon for Berwick. Archibald continued to support Henry, thus saving Tantallon from being attacked and burnt by Hertford's force which passed close by in May 1544.

When Hertford came back early in the following year, it is said that on his return southward he desecrated the tombs of the Douglases in Melrose Abbey, so causing Archibald to associate himself with the nationalist cause. In truth, the earl had changed his allegiance some months before, a shift perhaps not unrelated to his recent receipt of a Scottish pension amounting to £1000! His undoubted talents were now put to use for the good of Scotland and in February 1545 he led the army to victory over the English at Ancrum Moor, not far from his forebears' looted graves.

Thereafter, Archibald and Governor Arran co-existed, though neither trusted the other. The disaster at the battle of Pinkie, near Musselburgh, in September 1547, when Archibald, albeit reluctantly, led the charge against the English, has been blamed on their mutual lack of confidence. But Archibald and his castle at Tantallon continued to support the Scottish cause, and in 1548, during a naval engagement off Tantallon between a French and English fleet, 'the gunnarres of Temptalloun . . . schutand at the Inglishe schippis' and were rewarded with 14 shillings Scots. Archibald himself was honoured by being admitted to the Order of St Michael. In 1556, after an extraordinarily adventurous if somewhat devious political life, the sixth Douglas earl of Angus passed away peacefully within his castle at Tantallon.

A cast bronze hagbut bearing the arms and initials of James, earl of Arran, 1553. Guns like this were used mainly in the field, mounted on trestles. (In the collection of the Royal Museum of Scotland, Queen Street, Edinburgh: reproduced by kind permission of the National Museums of Scotland)

Tantallon back in crown hands

The passing of Archibald, the sixth earl, was the occasion for the crown to take the castle back into its custody. The death of the earl's nephew and heir, David, shortly after his uncle's and the fact that the new earl of Angus, Archibald, David's son, was a mere two years old was too golden an opportunity not to be missed in the light of Tantallon's recent contribution to the troubles that had beset the country. The castle was handed over to the keeping of the lord of Craigmillar and a detailed schedule of the munition and artillery equipment of the castle was made (see page 31).

In 1558 unspecified repairs were carried out, the timber for the building being despatched in John Dalmahoy's boats from Leith. Later that same year, six barrowmen were employed for ten days cleaning the draw-well within the inner close.

The keepership of the castle was changed frequently. George Drummond of Blair, when keeper, had a small garrison of seven horsemen and twenty-two foot soldiers; John Learmonth was in control in 1562. But in 1565 the eighth earl's uncle and tutor, James Douglas, fourth earl of Morton, took over the castle under an obligation that it should be 'reddie and patent to her majestie' as long as it was in his hands. Mary Queen of Scots, doubtless already fully aware of Morton's scheming on behalf of the Protestant cause, ordered the castle to be handed over to 'the lordis of the Bas elder and younger' and another inventory of the munition to be made. The queen herself visited Tantallon in November 1566.

When Archibald, the eighth earl, came of age, he became enmeshed in the intriguing affairs of his uncle, now Regent Morton. When Esme Stewart, earl of Lennox, and James Stewart, earl of Arran, directed the proceedings against Morton, which ultimately sealed his fate, Archibald removed all his valuables from his castles at Dalkeith and Aberdour to the far stronger fortalice at Tantallon and entered into treasonable negotiations with Queen

Portrait of James Douglas, 4th earl of Morton, uncle of Archibald, 8th earl of Angus. James Douglas, who later became Regent of Scotland, took over Tantallon Castle for a short time in 1565. This portrait has been attributed to Arnold Bronckorst, a Flemish painter who came to Scotland about 1578-9. (In the collection of the Scottish National Portrait Gallery: reproduced by kind permission of the Scottish National Galleries)

Elizabeth's ambassador, Thomas Randolph. Archibald was immediately proclaimed a traitor and shortly after Morton's execution in 1581, he went into exile in England.

Archibald was allowed to return in September 1582. Shortly afterwards, however, the king was informed that the earl was fortifying Tantallon, 'but at the end it was known to the king that he kept his house quietly and that he repaired the shackles of an old brewhouse without any other fortifications'. Archibald continued to spearhead the ultra-Protestant cause and a temporary banishment north of the Spey was soon followed by a further period of exile in England. Allowed home in 1584, he evidently continued to give cause for concern for the earl of Rothes was instructed to hold

Tantallon for the crown for almost two years. Archibald was restored to his estates in November 1585, but within three years, at the early age of thirty-four, he was dead, killed it was said by a disease attributed to an evil spell cast by one Agnes Sampson, who was condemned as a witch and burnt at the stake on the Castle Hill in Edinburgh.

With the eighth earl dead and his heir, William Douglas of Glenbervie, dying in 1591, the staunch Protestant stance of the earls of Angus came to an end. William, the tenth earl, was a committed Roman Catholic who had already suffered exile in 1589 for his religion. In an attempt to win back his inheritance, he embraced the Protestant faith but he proved only a lukewarm adherent and by 1593 had returned to Roman Catholicism. In 1608 he was excommunicated on the order of the king, imprisoned, then sent into exile to France. In his testament dated 31 October 1608, among other details, he ordained that 'mionitioun wapinis and airmour within the Castle of Thomptalloun remain within the said Castle'. He died in exile and was buried in the abbey church of St Germain-des-Prés, in Paris.

Tantallon and Cromwell

Those 'mionitioun wapinis and airmour' were not long in being put to use. Towards the close of 1650, a body of thirty horse, 'desperado gallants' or moss-troopers, as they became known, had established themselves within Tantallon's strong defences. Their attacks on Cromwell's lines of communication were so thorough and well-planned that it was reported to the Lord Protector that 'they had taken more men and done us more harm than the whole Scots army and all their garrisons'. In retaliation, General Monk, with a force numbering between two and three thousand men, was ordered to attack the stronghold. In February 1651, having first burnt the hamlet of Castleton and chased the defenders inside the castle, Monk was before the walls with a gun-battery of granadoes and six battering-pieces. The garrison numbered 91 officers and men, with 15 or 16 large guns and about 120 small arms. Monk's bombardment lasted twelve days. Sir James Balfour's narrative of the events continues: '. . . Capitane Alexander Setton defendit the same gallantly; bot after that the enimeyes canon had oppind a werey large breache, and filled the dray ditche with the wall, he entered it by storme. The Capitane and thesse few men (which) were with him, betooke themselves to (the) tower, and resolued to sell their lives at als good a rait as they could, if that quarter should (be) denayed them; bot the enimey seinng them stand gallantly to it, preferrid

General George Monk, duke of Albemarle, painted by Sir Peter Lely and studio. In 1651 General Monk attacked Tantallon with a force numbering between two and three thousand men. His twelve-day bombardment did a great deal of damage to the building. (In the collection of the Scottish National Portrait Gallery: reproduced by kind permission of the Scottish National Galleries)

them quarters, which they excepted.'

The devastation wrought by General Monk's artillery is plain to see. The derelict state of the masonry scarp wall at the outer ditch and the shattered stumps of the two terminal towers at the inner curtain are doubtless attributable to that murderous bombardment. That the great central gatehouse stands largely unmolested may be due to the presence of the ditched ravelin projecting beyond the outer ditch, a triangular earthwork where heavy guns were mounted so as to delay any frontal assault, by keeping the besiegers' artillery at a safe distance. The notion of an all-round bastioned artillery fortification had taken root before the 1651 siege, but Tantallon's siting rendered it incapable of being so developed. Far from being 'of suche strength' and 'unwinabill to any enemies', Tantallon was now shown to be extremely vulnerable. The castle's days as a fortress were over.

Tantallon abandoned

If Tantallon had still been viewed before the siege by the eleventh earl of Angus as an acceptable noble residence, which is doubtful, it is clear that the enormous battering which the place got in 1651 rendered it totally unserviceable. The earl, created marquis of Douglas, was by now residing more comfortably at Bothwell and Douglas Castles, both in Lanarkshire. Despite substantial alterations to the accommodation in the previous century, particularly noticeable in the free-standing hall block along the north side of the inner close, Tantallon was just as incapable of being upgraded into a seventeenth-century baronial residence as it was impossible to convert into an artillery fortification of the same period. An inventory of the contents of the castle, taken in 1670, makes forlorn reading (see page 31). In 1699 the castle and barony were purchased by Sir Hew Dalrymple, lord president of the Court of Session, who made no effort to make the place inhabitable and the structure was allowed to continue decaying.

At the close of the nineteenth century Sir Walter Hamilton Dalrymple did much to save the castle from decay and since 1924 when the guardianship of the building was taken over by the state, the whole fabric has been thoroughly overhauled. During the operations, a number of large stone shot, iron cannon balls, bombs and lead shot were unearthed. Among other relics found were medieval keys of iron, buckles, tags, mountings and chains of brass, foreign jettons (mostly of Nuremberg origin), coins and fragments of pottery. A selection of these articles can be seen in the Royal Museum of Scotland, Queen Street, Edinburgh.

An engraving of Tantallon Castle with the Bass Rock and the Isle of May by S Hooper (1789). (Reproduced by kind permission of the Royal Commission on the Ancient and Historical Monuments of Scotland)

The castle from the air, looking south-east. The great stone
curtain shields the close, or courtyard, at the end of the
promontory. In front is the outer ward, now bereft of all
buildings save a dovecot. The outer ditch, the pointed ravelin
and the outermost entrenchment (bottom right) are clearly
picked out by the rays of the setting sun.

'A great red curtain of stone'

The mighty stone castle that commands the headland is protected on three sides by sheer cliffs plunging dramatically into the waters far below. At the far end of the promontory the great red curtain of stone envelops the close (the 'cloiss' of 1556) around which was arranged the principal accommodation. The outer ward, housing lesser offices, defined from the outset by a substantial earthwork, lies in front of the curtain.

THE OUTWORKS

The castle can only be approached from the south-western side across the grassy headland. As we approach the castle, we can see how the original fourteenth-century defences have been reinforced in later years to improve the defensive capability of the castle, particularly from the more damaging effects of cannon-fire. Without archaeological excavation, we cannot say with certainty at what date the various outworks were constructed, though the broad outline seems clear enough.

The outermost **entrenchment** running northwards away from the present custodian's office is impossible to place in the sequence. It need not necessarily be a defensive feature, but may be an earthwork thrown up by an attacking force. One such force, in 1491, is known to have cut trenches during a siege.

The main outwork is a massive **outer ditch** with a high inner rampart of earth and a lower one along the counterscarp. From superficial evidence, it is clearly a work of more than one period, though it is likely to have been created at the outset to define the limit of the outer ward of William Douglas's castle. At some stage after the mid sixteenth century an earthen **ravelin**, a detached triangular gun-platform, was placed in front of the outer ditch, linked to the outer ward by two **traverses** crossing the ditch.

The entrance into the outer ward is at the eastern end of the outer ditch. The remnant of an **outer gate** survives, with evidence of a massive double door. The gate was further protected by the outer ditch itself, at this point cut through the bedrock, and on its seaward side by a masonry **traverse wall** which terminated in a round two-storeyed **tower**. These features, with their horizontal wide-mouthed gunholes, are of sixteenth-century date and with good reason can be held to have been built on the orders of Archibald, the sixth earl, a little before the siege of 1528. The tower and traverse wall both show evidence of repair to damage, probably caused by bombardment, and those repairs have been largely carried out in the greenish stone which, as we will see in the castle proper, is a characteristic feature of the work done for the crown between 1528 and 1543. In addition to repair work, the rock-cut ditch immediately in front of the outer gate and traverse wall was deepened and a further gunhole incorporated in the extended traverse wall foundation. The masonry **scarp** protecting the rampart behind the outer ditch to the left of the gateway is constructed in the same greenish stone and may also be part of the defensive measures carried out for the crown. Its present advanced state of ruin is most likely attributable to General Monk's devastating artillery bombardment of 1651.

The **outer ward** is now devoid of buildings other than a **dovecot** of seventeenth-century lectern type. South of this, foundations of outhouse buildings of late date have been found. No doubt further archaeological investigation would find traces of other earlier buildings that would once have crowded this now bare and open outer ward. Two human skeletons, buried east and west,

View along the outer ditch towards the gunholed traverse wall and tower protecting the outer gate. On the left, the masonry scarp fronting the rampart of the outer ward (now in part subsided). On the right, the counterscarp.

were found behind the traverse wall and close to the cliff edge. This suggests that this part had been used as a burial ground, possibly during a period of siege.

The castle from the south. In the foreground is the outer gate, once arched over and fitted with a massive double door.

THE EXTERIOR

The most important and most conspicuous element in Tantallon's defence throughout its long history was the awesome curtain of sandstone drawn across the neck of the grassy headland. Impressively solid, with walls some 3.7 m thick, it has now a somewhat careworn appearance, having been battered not only by cannon but by the winds and storms that are as much a part of this exposed spot as the rugged cliffs themselves. The brute frontal mass of the curtain is scarcely relieved by the few narrow slits lighting the mural chambers and access stairs behind. Also, when first built, the walls were finished at the top with plain parapets, adding to the severity of the castle's outward appearance. The present crenellated parapets nestling on continuous corbelling belong to the post-1528 alterations.

The great curtain was furnished with projecting towers, a Mid Tower centrally placed and two terminal towers, the Douglas Tower on the far left and the East Tower over to the right. The three towers together housed the principal lodgings of the lord, his constable, or keeper of the castle, and others in his household. Sadly, little survives of the two terminal towers, their 'innards' having been ripped out most likely by General Monk's artillery in 1651. The Mid Tower, in contrast, stands reasonably intact, though its somewhat crude appearance is due entirely to it having been radically altered after 1528.

Immediately in front of the great curtain a broad and deep rock-cut ditch extends right across the promontory from cliff to cliff, enhancing the huge scale of the towering walls. As built, the castle was intended to be capable of being defended by a relatively small garrison stationed in the main at the wall head. From this vantage point and armed with hand-weapons and larger artillery pieces (not cannon but machines hurling stones and other projectiles) they could confidently expect to keep a besieging force at a reasonably safe distance. Should the attacking force break through the outer defences, however, the gaping inner ditch presented a further considerable obstacle to the pioneers charged with creating a breach in the curtain.

The castle from the north-west, with the shattered stump of the Douglas Tower on the left. Centre right, the Mid Tower rises up from behind the Fore Tower. At the far end is the ruined East Tower. The three towers together housed the main accommodation.

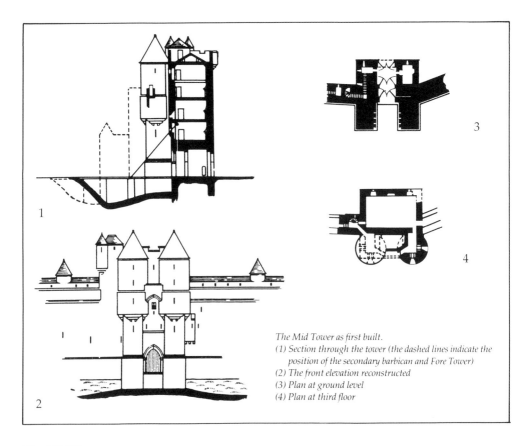

The Mid Tower as first built.
(1) Section through the tower (the dashed lines indicate the position of the secondary barbican and Fore Tower)
(2) The front elevation reconstructed
(3) Plan at ground level
(4) Plan at third floor

The Mid Tower

The Mid Tower, incorporating the gatehouse and entry to the close, stands almost entire. It has, however, been changed so comprehensively over the years that at first sight it presents a most confusing picture. The alterations have largely been confined to the most vulnerable, outward-facing part. It would be best first to describe the Mid Tower as it was originally built, and then to demonstrate how it came to assume its present appearance. It would help if we put from our mind for the moment the obvious greenish stone with red freestone bands and the existing narrow entrance doorway for they belong to the post-1528 crown repairs.

The Mid Tower was conceived as a great keep-gatehouse. That is to say, its lofty five-storeyed height incorporated private lodgings in the upper four floors above a portal and vaulted entrance passage. The upper storeys were reached by a spiral stair (since blocked up) entered off the north side of the entrance passage. Each storey comprised a single room floored with wood. Good-sized canopied fireplaces can be seen in each room, the lower three set into the wall nearest the close and the topmost in the opposite wall. Small chambers and latrine closets have been carved out of the adjacent east curtain and the forework projecting out from the gatehouse (see opposite). The generous proportions of the rooms and their elegant fireplaces indicate that these were sophisticated apartments, and one of them at least is likely to have served as the hall and chamber (the lodging) of the lord's constable, who was charged with keeping the castle in good order and well provisioned.

18

The upper storeys within the Mid Tower, with their canopied fireplaces.

The **portal** and **entrance passage** at ground level have been well protected. The portal itself, a finely-moulded and pointed arch, has vertical grooves for a portcullis that would normally have been housed in the chamber overhead. In front of the portal was a drawbridge, placed over a deep pit, and worked by chains from the same overhead chamber. The holes through which the chains threaded are just visible over the portal. Behind the portal and within the entrance passage were positioned three two-leafed doors or iron yetts, one at either end of the passage and the third about midway along. The two nearest the portal were further secured by massive timber draw-bars. The slots which housed them can be seen in the side walls. On the south side of the passage is a vaulted chamber with evidence for a fireplace in the back wall. This was the **guard-room** or porter's lodge.

When first built, the Mid Tower was given a forework of twin jambs, or spine walls,

The original outer portal into the castle, with the Mid Tower behind.

A mural chamber in the upper part of the Mid Tower. The window, with its stone benches still in place, was subsequently blocked when the Fore Tower was built against it after the 1528 siege.

19

One of two corbelled turrets high up on the forework of the Mid Tower. The rectangular opening in the corbelling, called a machicolation, was a defensive feature enabling the garrison to cover the wall base from a comparatively safe position in one of the mural chambers (see page 19).

The surviving fragment of barbican emerges from the base of the later Fore Tower like two raking supports.

projecting into the rock-cut ditch. These jambs were rectangular in plan until they reached the level of the second storey of the Mid Tower; above this they were corbelled out into rounded turrets which continued up through the remaining height of the building. On each face the corbelling had a central opening called a machicolation, a defensive feature which enabled the garrison to cover the wall bases from a comparatively safe position. At the level of the third storey the turrets were linked by a narrow bridge carried on a pointed arch. In addition to these defensive provisions at the upper levels of the jambs, the wall-head of the Mid Tower itself was furnished with an embattled parapet. At either corner, overlooking the inner close, there was a small projecting turret, and midway between these, directly over the inner portal, the remnant of a projecting box-machicolation.

This then was how the Mid Tower looked when first built. At a later date, perhaps around the turn of the fourteenth and fifteenth centuries, construction work was carried out to improve substantially the capacity of the Mid Tower to withstand an attack. The ditch was widened and a **barbican**, of which only a fragment now remains, was built immediately in front of the Mid Tower to strengthen the defence of the entrance. The gateway into the castle, together with its drawbridge, were then brought forward a distance of some 12 m. The barbican had three levels. In the middle of the sandwich was the gateway and entrance passage, partly floored in wood. Beneath was a pit, entered either from within the barbican down steps crudely cut out of the sloping scarp of the rock, or from the ditch itself through two round-headed doorways. The top level of the barbican, its fighting

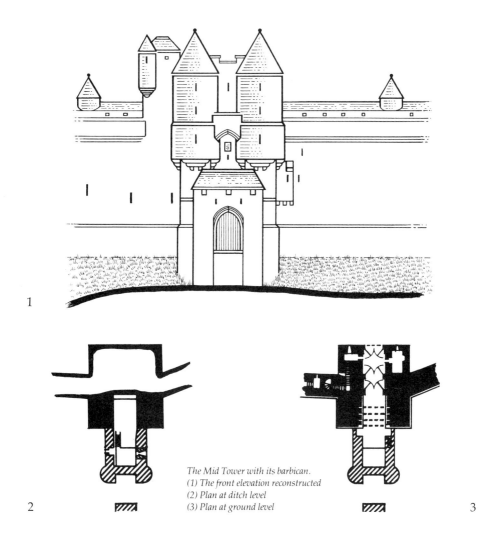

1

2

3

The Mid Tower with its barbican.
(1) The front elevation reconstructed
(2) Plan at ditch level
(3) Plan at ground level

platform, was reached by a mural stair in the east wall.

It is clear that, whatever other damage may have been done to the castle in the course of the siege of 1528, the Mid Tower, and in particular the barbican fronting it, suffered substantially. The upper part of the original forework and a greater portion of the barbican either collapsed or were pulled down to clear the way for a major remodelling of the Mid Tower's frontal defence. The work, carried out for the crown, continued in progress from 1529 to at least 1539 when the Master of Works' accounts show building work in progress under the master mason, George Sempill. It is just possible that the work was completed after the earl of Angus's return from exile in 1543 for the coat of arms within the stone panel high up on the outer face of the new build, though now badly weathered, is his.

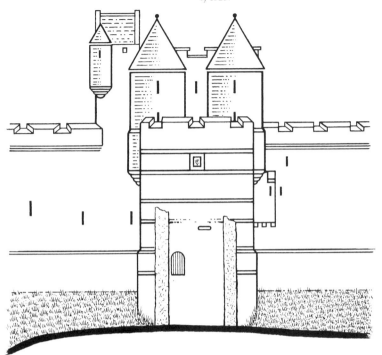

The Fore Tower

The new Fore Tower (the 'foir tour' of 1556) was designed for cannon against cannon. A massive wall with rounded corners, built of greenish stone divided horizontally by bands of red, was built over the stump of the barbican and laid against the battered face of the original forework, virtually burying both. The portal was brought forward some 3.5 m and drastically reduced in width, leaving room now only for the passage of foot traffic where once horse and wagon could pass through with ease. The entrance passage behind was similarly reduced in width and fitted with several doors. The portal at the rear of the Mid Tower leading into the close was narrowed at the same time.

Wide-mouthed **gunholes** were inserted at strategic points. Three were placed close to the portal, one on either side flanking the inner ditch and the third 'abone the brig', that is directly over the portal and commanding the bridge over the inner ditch.

The basement of the barbican was retained, though both doorways leading into the ditch were blocked and given wide-mouthed gunholes also. The Fore Tower was carried up to the wall-walk level. The high bridge linking the jambs was hidden and the void between them completely packed with masonry. There is no evidence to show how the wall-top of the Fore Tower was finished in stone, but by the time of General Monk's siege, the guns mounted here were protected by a turf rampart.

One of numerous wide-mouthed gunholes incorporated into the Fore Tower.

THE CLOSE

Passing through the Mid Tower we enter the **close**, a good-sized courtyard that today gives a misleading impression of openness but which in its day was hemmed in by stone and timber buildings. The great curtain of stone was originally intended to be drawn around all four sides of the enclosure, but apparently the scheme for the south and east sides was never carried through. The stone footings of the uncompleted **sea gate**, though, still cling to the eastern edge.

The main lodgings of the lord and his household were contained within the three towers in the west, landward curtain. Along the north side is a **hall block**, the principal banqueting suite. Close by the Mid Tower is the **well**, circular in shape and sunk in the rock to a depth of over 32 m. This feature was discovered at the end of the nineteenth century by Sir Walter Hamilton Dalrymple, the then owner, and cleared out at that time. Against the main curtain, either side of the Mid Tower, were **lean-to buildings** of uncertain function. That to the south of the Mid Tower was gabled and provided small chambers and a long loft. It was later raised and an additional floor inserted. One of these 'toofalls' may have served as the 'munition houss' in the sixteenth century.

The close, or courtyard, from the south-east, with the foundations of the never-completed sea gate in the right foreground.

The East Tower

The East Tower, D-shaped in plan, originally contained five storeys floored in wood. Each floor had a single chamber entered from a spiral stair on the north side, with that on the ground floor entered separately from the close. Latrine closets and fireplaces for each chamber were in the south wall, which has largely gone, and all we have now are windows fitted with stone seats. The ground storey, however, remains reasonably intact. In the third-floor chamber is a doorway intended to give access to the wall-walk on the south curtain which was never completed. The only remaining window in this chamber has at one time been barred on the outside with an iron grille and may have served as a place of confinement for persons of noble birth. Petty criminals from the locality were more grimly incarcerated in the pit-prison (see page 26). The topmost chamber was vaulted and the platform roof of the tower had a corbelled and embattled parapet.

In the rebuilding programme following the 1528 siege, this tower was substantially altered and strengthened. The bottom three storeys were reduced to two, the old wooden floors replaced by heavy stone vaults, and wide-mouthed gunholes with throats up to 400 mm in diameter were punched through the landward-facing wall, which was increased to a thickness of 4.5 m. This new work is recognisable by the characteristic greenish stone.

The rear of a wide-mouthed gunhole (see page 22) in the ground storey of the East Tower. The gun would have been a stocked forged-iron breech loader mounted on a trestle (see page 9).

The curtain wall

By entering the doorway immediately south of the Mid Tower, we can make our way to the battlements. The first **stair** is a straight flight made remarkable by its ceiling, a continuous and attractive arrangement of transverse arches. Thereafter a **spiral stair** takes us up to the battlements. The stairs are ill-lit by narrow slits to landward and small windows looking on to the close. Off the stairways are small chambers carved out of the wall, devoid of features other than a window. After 1528 these chambers were packed with masonry to increase the wall's capacity to withstand cannon bombardment. Some of this 'massie work' was removed at the end of the nineteenth century, but where it has been retained we see that characteristic greenish stone.

One of two mural stairs in the curtain, with its attractive arrangement of continuous transverse arches.

The top of the Fore Tower. In the centre, one of the two rounded turrets from the original forework (see page 20) immured in the subsequent post-1528 infilling. The narrow flying bridge linking the two turrets (see page 18) is visible in the foreground.

Left: View from the Fore Tower looking towards the shattered East Tower. The crenellated parapet atop the curtain, carried on continuous corbelling, was built after the 1528 siege and designed for use with hand-held guns resting on the crenels. The heaviest gun-pieces (see page 8) were mounted on carriages at the wall-heads of the three towers.

The **battlements** were altered following the infilling of the mural chambers beneath. We can only guess at the original arrangement, but it seems likely that there was a narrow wall-walk flanked by crenellated parapet walls and possibly roofed over. The post-1528 work resulted in the crenellated parapet carried on continuous corbelling that we see on the landward face today. The crenels would have been suitable for use with hand-held guns, with the heavier armament emplaced on the wall-heads of the three towers.

By walking along the battlements, we pass through the penultimate storey of the Mid Tower and note the outline of the flying bridge formerly linking the two jambs of the first forework before the void was packed with masonry after 1528. The defensive elements at the tower head already noted (page 20) can now be seen at close quarters; namely the corbelled turrets projecting from the two corners overlooking the close and the vestige of a box-machicolation positioned directly over the inner portal of the gatehouse.

Continuing through the Mid Tower we reach the battlements atop the northern stretch of curtain, identical to the stretch over the south curtain, and descending the spiral stair we encounter a situation similar to that in the other mural stair. Again, some of the 'massie work' has been taken out of the mural chambers. Emerging into the close again, we find the doorway partially blocked by a secondary stair-tower built to replace the old spiral stair within the Mid Tower. The replacement stair is constructed in that familiar greenish stone, identifying it as part of the post-1528 work. The masons, however, failed to tie their new build back into the original masonry and as a consequence the tower has parted company with the curtain.

View northwards from the East Tower. On the left is the Mid Tower, with the Douglas Tower and its adjacent hall block in the background.

The Douglas Tower

The great circular tower at the northern end of the curtain wall, referred to as the 'Douglass tour' in 1556, is now sadly only a mere fragment. But both on account of its name, and also because of its great girth and undoubted former sophistication, it may be assumed with confidence to have been the private lodging of the Douglas earls of Angus. The close proximity of the banqueting-hall to this tower may be deemed to reinforce this association. The tower contained six storeys above a vaulted basement. Each was floored with wood and comprised a single chamber with an attached vaulted latrine closet. The topmost chamber was vaulted and the tower-head fortified. The five upper storeys were reached by a spiral stair in the adjacent curtain; those on the ground floor and in the basement were entered directly off the close.

The basement housed a **pit-prison** on a level considerably below that of the close. Reached by a narrow mural stair, it has a floor of solid rock and only a narrow shaft for ventilation. A second narrow stair and passage in the north-east angle lead to a latrine. This unwholesome place of internment was used by the lord of Tantallon, who had responsibility for the maintenance of law and order ('pit and gallows') within the barony, for the incarceration of those unfortunate wretches who had, or were suspected of having, fallen foul of the law. Few of their names are known to us, though the likes of James Rannald and Johnne Mitchell, two merchants warded in the castle in 1584 on unspecified charges, may be typical of the sorts of people so confined. The more high-born personages warded here — the duchess of Albany in 1425, for example, or Alexander, lord of the Isles, four years later — would have been more comfortably restrained in one of the towers. The fact that the window overlooking the close from the third floor of the East Tower has had an iron grille sealing it suggests perhaps that this may have served as a place of imprisonment also.

The hall block

The stone range along the north side of the close adjacent to the Douglas Tower has had a long and varied, if somewhat confusing, history. It began as a hall block, free-standing and apparently only half the present length, the eastern half being added later. On each of the two floors was a hall, a lower or 'laigh hall' at ground level and an upper or 'great hall' above. Both halls, measuring some 17 m by 7 m, functioned as reception suites; the difference between them was one of degree.

The great hall was superior and accordingly has been more graciously handled by the builder. Generous windows down both sides brought adequate light and ventilation into the chamber, the courtyard elevation having a second row of smaller pointed windows at a higher level, bringing light into the open-timbered roof, whose outline can be seen impressed into the west gable. The

In the great hall looking westwards towards the Douglas Tower. The fine open-timbered roof has left its imprint high up in the gable. The blocked-up spiral stair to the upper gallery is in the right-hand corner.

hall was heated by a broad fireplace midway along the north wall. Access was from a doorway in the west gable, reached originally by a stair rising from the close. Over the doorway there may well have been a musicians' gallery reached by a spiral stair, later blocked, which can just be made out in the north-west corner. The upper door at the level of the gallery, though blocked, can also be seen. If this is the case, the top, or dais, end of the hall was at the far, eastern end and there is clear evidence that a good-sized window overlooked the close here. This is now greatly altered but in its original state would have been able to bathe the top table, or 'hie burde', in plentiful sunshine.

The laigh hall was handled in a more humble manner, reflecting its subservient role. It lacked the high roof and the windows were less generously sized. But the fireplace was capacious enough and placed in an identical position to that in the great hall. Close by was a latrine closet. Access to this hall was through the south wall by a doorway (immediately to the left of the present doorway) that has subsequently been converted into a window. A deep square slot in the west jamb shows that it was well defended by a timber draw-bar.

Down the years, this hall block underwent substantial change, reflecting well the changing nature of society in Scotland as she passed from the medieval feudal age into the modern era with its notions of increased privacy and etiquette. We cannot say precisely when the changes began to be made to the hall block for there is no documentation recording the alterations; neither can they be associated with the various alterations to the castle's defences. But the characteristic greenish stone that has been used in the building of the eastern extension to the hall suggests that this was part of the post-1528 programme. At any event, they must have been initiated before the 1556 inventory was drawn up (page 31).

The laigh hall may have been the first to be altered. Three vaulted cellars ('volts') were inserted, joined by a vaulted alley running the length of the block with doorways at either end and a new doorway inserted in the south wall, more centrally placed than the earlier entrance to its left.

The great hall above was divided into two floors, the lower floor continuing to function as a hall (it is still called the 'lang hall' in the 1670 inventory), though the importance of such a chamber by this time had greatly declined from the banqueting suite of former times. Access into it was still through the west gable but the outside forestair, possibly of timber, was removed and the gap between the hall block and the Douglas Tower was infilled with a vaulted masonry construction supporting both a stair up from the close as well as a direct link with the Douglas Tower. Part of the north curtain wall was cut down to form a window lighting this lobby. The upper floor, the 'hall loft' of 1556, was reached from the west side also but at a higher level, giving a direct link into the Douglas Tower at the fourth of its seven storeys. It was then that the spiral stair in the north-west corner of the great hall was closed up.

This was not the end of the story. The hall block was extended eastward by as much again. Little survives of this addition except the ground floor, divided into three vaulted rooms, one of which was the **kitchen**, and another the **bakehouse**. The third, by analogy with castles elsewhere, would have served as the **brewhouse**. The kitchen has two fireplaces, one containing an oven and slop-drain. The bakehouse has two ovens contained within a small outbuilding through the north wall. The larger oven was lined with marine stone from North Berwick and the throat of the other retains fragments of tile lining. There is evidence of another fireplace in the east wall of the brewhouse.

This eastern extension was given at least one more storey which has now almost entirely gone. Access was from a spiral forestair in the close. Whatever form the upper structure took, its construction evidently caused further alterations to the great hall and loft adjacent. The double corbels inserted into the side walls to support the loft were cloured away and new single corbels positioned at a higher level. These still remain. In this way, the great hall ceiling was raised again, though to nothing like its former height. The size of the hall loft was consequently reduced in height. With the great hall taller, the windows overlooking the close were heightened and so enlarged. It is this room which is described as the 'lang hall' in the inventory of 1670, and we may assume,

The seaward end of the hall block with the remains of the kitchen, bakehouse and brewhouse. In the background, the Bass Rock.

by a process of elimination, that the 'dyneing roume' and 'the chamber caled my ladie's chamber' once occupied the now missing first floor in the extension, possibly along with other private chambers.

By this late date it is clear that the remodelled hall block with its eastern extension had been serving for quite some time as the principal lordly apartment within the entire castle. A single 'chamber in Douglas tower' is mentioned, and though the devastating bombardment from General Monk's artillery doubtless put an end to all thought of continuing in occupation of it, the awkwardly-sited, ill-suited accommodation it provided, built for a baron some three hundred years earlier, had evidently fallen out of favour. And though the hall block itself may have given sufficient dignified living space at this late date, the exposed headland on which it perched ill became a noble family of Charles II's day. The 1670 inventory 'of the plenishing in Tantallon Castle' makes depressing reading (page 31). Much of the furniture is described as old and entries like that for the 'out roume of the garden chamber' betoken a once mighty castle fallen from grace:

> 'In the . . . roume . . . thir is ane bedstead, wanteing (lacking) cover above, with ane kist (chest); ther is ane old caise in the window with sum broken glese.'

IN THE VICINITY OF THE CASTLE

Haven
On the rocks underlying the north cliff of the promontory on which the castle stands are a series of **post-holes** and the remains of a **breakwater**, all that is left of the haven referred to in a document of the year 1565, when the earl of Morton was designated 'Keeper of the Haven of Thomptalloun'.

Crane-bastion
The ruin of a **crane-bastion** overlooking the bay and the ox-road is to be seen on the cliff top, 183 m south-south-east of the outer gate. This was a winching mechanism used for hauling provisions up to the headland from boats anchored below. There was probably another one sited at the sea gate within the castle.

Tantallon castle from the south, with the remains of the crane-bastion sited on top of the cliff in the foreground.

Tantallon Castle from the north-west, with the 'Haven of Thomptalloun' directly below.

'Tantallon—fortress and residence'

Amongst the extensive documentation charting the story of Tantallon and its owners are two inventories which together give us a most interesting glimpse into the two roles the castle was intended to serve. One details the 'mvnition and artaillerie', drawn up in 1556, the other catalogues the 'plenishing' (the furnishings, fixtures and fittings) there in 1670.

The inventory of the 'mvnition and artaillerie being in the house and castell of Thomtalloun' was taken by the then keeper, the laird of Craigmillar, for his sovereign, Mary Queen of Scots. The schedule shows how well stocked the castle was with guns, other weapons and their accoutrements at a particularly crucial time in its history.

The largest gun-pieces were mounted at strategic parts of the castle, including the battlements at the top of the East Tower, the Fore Tower and the Douglas Tower. The smaller guns were emplaced within the close and directly over the drawbridge ('abone the brig'). Other weapons, principally pikes and halberds, were stacked in readiness at the gate, in the entrance passage and within the Mid Tower. The remainder of the guns, together with the other weaponry and assorted accoutrements — barrels of powder, powder horns and iron bullets — were in store in various places, including the munition house, the workhouse, the vaults and cellars beneath the hall and the loft above the hall.

The inventory of the 'plenishing', taken as it was in 1670, shows the castle very much in the twilight of its days as a residence of nobility. It is not easy from this distance in time to relate some of the chambers mentioned in the schedule to particular rooms in the castle. Where, for instance, were the 'out roume of the garden chamber', and the 'reid' and 'blew' chambers? What is perfectly clear is that much of the original accommodation within the East, Mid and Douglas towers was no longer in use by this late date. And what there is in the way of furniture is apparently antiquated. The 'chamber in Dowglas towere' has 'ane ald bedstead', 'stanchellis' (stanchions) in the south window, and 'ane caise and broades' (casement and shutters) in the north, with 'ane ald table'.

It is the hall block that has obviously been the nucleus of the lordly accommodation for some time. We have references to the 'lang hall', the 'dyneing roume' and 'the chamber caled my ladie's chamber', all reasonably well furnished. The dining room, for example, has 'four carpit chyres (chairs), ane ald armed chyre, ane bedstead, ane bathing fatt (tub), with ane studie and three fixed windowes, with broades and glasse, and ane wainscott table'. But the signs of disuse are there too. 'In the baikhouse ther is onlie ane table' does not suggest any great hive of activity. Neither is the stable accommodation bursting at the seams — it can only boast 'ane heck (rack) and ane manger'.

W Fraser, *The Douglas Book* (Edinburgh 1885).
G Donaldson (ed), *The Edinburgh History of Scotland*, 4 vols (Edinburgh 1975).
I MacIvor, 'Artillery and Major Places of Strength in the Lothians and the East Border, 1513-42', in D Caldwell (ed), *Scottish Weapons & Fortifications. 1100-1800* (Edinburgh 1981).
C J Tabraham, *Scottish Castles and Fortifications* (Edinburgh 1986).
S Cruden, *The Scottish Castle* (Edinburgh 1981).

ISBN 0 11 492500 3

Printed in Scotland for HMSO by McQueen Ltd., Galashiels. Dd. 0762196 C57·5 9/86